Guidebook for

State Rehabilitation Council

Chairpersons,

Members and Administrators

National Coalition of Rehabilitation Councils (NCSRC)
www.ncsrc.net

Please use the following citation when referencing, reproducing, or utilizing information obtained from this resource.

National Coalition of State Rehabilitation Councils (NCSRC) (2019). *Guidebook for SRC Chairpersons, Members and Administrators- www.NCSRC.net.*

Table of Contents

Acknowledgements

On behalf of the National Coalition of State Rehabilitation Councils (NCSRC) we would like to thank the many contributors to the content of this Guidebook. The many examples, promising practices, ideas, tools, and strategies shared within this guidebook came from numerous SRCs and guests who spoke to us during webinars, teleconferences, and on-location conference trainings.

Should you need additional information, please contact us. We hope you will take the time to view and share with your SRC and/or VR colleagues whenever there is an opportunity for member orientation, continuing education, strengthening partnerships and collaboration. The NCSRC looks forward to receiving your feedback on the usefulness of the guide.

Introduction and History of State Vocational Rehabilitation Councils

When the Rehabilitation Act Amendments were being considered by the 102nd Congress in 1992, disability rights activism had increased and recommended changes to the Rehabilitation Act that included persons with disabilities be at the table. As a result, Revisions to the act included individual dignity, self-determination, inclusion and full participation of persons with disabilities. In addition, this included the establishment of a State Rehabilitation Advisory Council with a majority of the members (51%) being persons with disabilities.

By the 1998 Amendments, SRC's role and empowerment were recognized and strengthened. The name and role of the body of advocates was changed from the State Rehabilitation Advisory Council to the State Rehabilitation Council. The role changed from being advisory, to being involved in developing policies, planning activities, evaluation the program effectiveness and carrying out other functions related to the vocational rehabilitation program. This also included that the SRC, in conjunction with the VR agency, jointly conduct the comprehensive needs assessment of individuals with disabilities in the state, develop (and agree to) the State's annual goals and priorities, and evaluate the VR performance toward the goals annually. The role of the SRC changed from advisory to working in partnership with the State VR agency.

Section 105 of the Rehabilitation Act of 1973 (as amended) requires consumers, advocates and other representatives of individuals with disabilities to participate in the administration and oversight of a state's VR program. The SRC fulfills this mandate in all states and territories. This is required in order for Vocational Rehabilitation programs to be eligible for and maintain federal VR funds. The SRC must consist of at least fifteen (15) members. They cannot have less unless they are a commission. There is not a maximum number of members unless Council Bylaws note otherwise. Members are appointed by the Governor, representing a variety of perspectives from the VR program and disability community as outlined in the legislation.

Members can serve up to two consecutive three year terms. The SRC must conduct no less than four (4) quarterly meetings throughout the year. The general public will be provided with notice of the meetings in accordance with the state or territory's Open Meeting Act. The SRC's responsibilities and activities include:

☐ Unified or Combined State Plan: The SRC advises the agency on the development of the VR Services Portion of the State Plan. The SRC and agency should partner to develop, agree to and review the plan's goals and priorities of the agency.

☐ Comprehensive Statewide Needs Assessment: To identify and assess the needs of individuals with disabilities, the SRC collaborates with agency staff on the Comprehensive Statewide Needs Assessment, which is completed every three years.

☐ Policy Consultation: The Council should have a significant role in the development, understanding and implementation of the agency's policies and procedures. Any significant policies that impact the consumer must be brought before the Council for discussion. This is part of the SRC mission and responsibility.

The agency should provide detailed information to the Council members on why the policy is needed, the implication of any change in a written policy, reasoning if a policy is being deleted or amended.

This should be a routine portion of the agenda for each Council meeting.

☐ Consumer Satisfaction Surveys: The SRC must be an integral partner with their agency to assist in the development and dissemination of the Consumer Satisfaction Surveys. The Council should be given a written evaluation of those surveys results and provide follow-up feedback.

☐ Evaluation and Recommendations: The SRC reviews, analyzes and evaluates the performance of VR programs. A particular focus is given to eligibility, service provision, and activities that impact employment outcomes. As a result of this process, the SRC adopts recommendations which are submitted to their agency for serious consideration.

☐ Coordination and Participation: The SRC actively engages with other councils and advisory bodies to enhance the number of individuals served. SRC members also are encouraged to participate in work groups, public meetings and stakeholder forums.

The most important responsibility of the State Rehabilitation Councils is to advise, make recommendations and assist your state or territory in preparing their State Plan for Vocational Services. The overall purpose of the State Plan is to assure that State and Federal governments play a leadership role in promoting employment for persons with disabilities and to ensure a link between citizen participation and the legislative process.

A primary goal should be to ensure that people with disabilities are provided with an equal opportunity to receive the programs, services and supports needed. We should work diligently in our pursuit for consumer satisfaction and ways in which services can be improved or developed while striving to achieve the mission, vision and goals of the Council and agency.

The Council does not assist in the resolution of any individual case issues. The role of the State Rehabilitation Council is clearly outlined under the Rehabilitation Act of 1973 and the Workforce Investment & Opportunity Act of 2014, addressing some of these areas:

Eligibility & Order of Selection (OOS)

Extent, Scope, & Effectiveness of Services

Functions affecting individual achievement of employment outcomes

Applications, reports, & evaluations.

Develop, agree to, & review state goals & priorities.

Evaluate effectiveness of VR program & submit progress reports to the Commissioner of the Rehabilitation Services Administration (RSA).

Advise & assist in the preparation of the State Plan portion of the Unified or Combined State Plan, & Amendments: the applications, reports, needs assessments, & evaluations.

Participate in Statewide Needs Assessment every 3-years.

This guidebook is designed to increase understanding of common issues for SRCs. The individuals utilizing the information in this manual may be the Council chairpersons, their fellow Governor-appointed Council members, SRC staff and pertinent VR staff. Topics that will be covered will include—

☐ Laws and regulations that define and guide the SRC;

☐ Collaborating with VR;

☐ Building partnerships with other disability councils and organizations;

☐ Assessing the needs of the state or territory;

☐ Recruiting, appointments, training, and supporting council member;

☐ Conducting effective outreach;

☐ Resource development.

Having a good understanding of the SRC not only to actively and effectively contribute is essential for the SRC leadership, members, and staff to assist in enhancing the VR services in each state and territory. Every person involved has a vital role in fostering the successful and efficient functioning of the SRC. Whether you are a new or long-time member or staff person, this manual was designed to give those involved a better understanding of the responsibilities of the SRC.

FOUNDING OF THE NATIONAL COALITION OF STATE REHABILITATION COUNCILS (NCSRC)

In November 2005, a handful of people affiliated with State Rehabilitation Councils shared lunch during the Conference of State Administrators of Vocational Rehabilitation (CSAVR) Conference in San Diego. We began considering the benefits and drawbacks of establishing a national organization. Those present were not elite. Like many of you, some were Governor-appointed volunteers serving on their respective Councils; others were staff with the sole responsibility of working for a Council; and others were agency staff assigned to provide support to their SRC. As a result of tenacious commitment by several SRCs, the hard work became a realization in October at the CSAVR 2007 Fall Conference held in San Antonio, Texas.

Several of those seated around the table were fortunate to serve on well-resourced Councils; while others had no budget. There were representatives from states and territories with either general and Blind programs or combined programs. Despite our notable differences, we had a great deal in common. What began as a "session" during the CSAVR conferences has now evolved to two days of intense trainings for SRCs, a website designed to support SRCs with the tools needed to assist in developing, networking and strengthening SRCs to reach their maximum potential.

Common ground and the power of our collective potential is what led a motivated core of individuals to move us from brainstorming to organizing. A Board of Directors was formed having representation from numerous states and territories making a commitment to develop a network for SRCs. With the support of the Rehabilitation Services Administration, national conference calls for all State Rehabilitation Councils have convened regularly on a bi-monthly basis. In addition, the NCSRC Board of Directors meets on a regular basis to further the structure and development of the NCSRC and to plan the spring and fall conferences. The Board of Directors meets on the

Friday before the fall conference to assess the progress of the NCSRC and formalize the direction of the NCSRC based on the evaluations that attendees complete at each conference to assure areas of need are covered.

NCSRC Website & List Serve

The Board of Directors has worked diligently with a consultant to create a more inclusive website that was be launched in November 2018 (**www.ncsrc.net**) that will also have the capability to link a user to any SRC or the NCSRC Board of Directors. This is a website for your Council ~ to keep training materials available for your convenience and use. You are welcome to utilize the conference power points or other information on the website for the enrichment of your Council.

This website allows SRCs to request information that can be sent to the list serve for input. If your Council is needing information, guidance or data, requests may be placed on the site and will be forwarded to all SRCs. To assure the list serve is kept current, the NCSRC Board of Directors asks that Councils make sure the names and contact information for the chairperson and VR appointed liaison are sent to the NCSRC website.

NCSRC Training Conferences

In partnership and coinciding with the Conference of State Administrators of Vocational Rehabilitation (CSAVR) spring and fall conferences, the NCSRC conducts two full days of training for SRC members on Saturday and Sunday.

SRCs are highly encouraged to request funding from their respective agencies to attend the national conferences to help educate their members in the role of the Council and broaden their knowledge of responsibilities and mandates. The result is seen in a foundation already being built which will position all of us to be more effective within our respective states and as a national entity.

The training topics are designed based on the evaluations from previous conferences and suggestions from SRCs. The CEO from CSAVR is always invited to give those attending an update on events in Washington, DC as well as keeping SRCs abreast of CSAVR activities. Guest speakers have also been significant to assist SRCs in achieving their highest goals and fulfilling their missions.

At each spring and fall CSAVR Conference, the Saturday and Sunday NCSRC sessions have focused on many topics to enable and empower SRCs to become more informed, form a network for resources and tools to help strengthen their Councils. Some of the areas that have been highlighted over the years have included: best practices, strategic planning and leadership enhancement, building stronger rapports with VR agencies, creating strong mission and vision statements, core values, SRC 101, understanding WIOA, SRC leadership, committee development and writing bylaws.

A fee is charged for these conferences to cover the costs of the hotel (meeting room, audio equipment, printed materials, etc.) Details regarding conferences are posted on the NCSRC website. Making hotel reservation early is strongly suggested.

All power point presentations and documents used during these trainings are available on the website within a few days following the conference for SRCs to use at their discretion.

NCSRC Conference Calls

National conference calls with topics requested by SRC members are conducted quarterly (March, June, September & December) with the dates of the calls. Calls will begin at 2:30 p.m. Eastern Time and normally last about one (1) hour. Any SRC member or VR liaison may participate in the calls. Generally, the Rehabilitation Services Administration (RSA) staff liaison for the SRCs participates on the call and provides an agency update.

The toll-free number is posted on the NCSRC website along with topics to be discussed. Notice of the meetings will be emailed to SRC Chairpersons and VR liaisons prior to the date of the call for information to be forwarded to their members to participate in the calls.

The Rehabilitation Act is found in the Workforce Innovation and Opportunity Act (WIOA)

WIOA is designed to strengthen and improve the nation's public workforce development system by helping Americans with barriers to employment, including individuals with disabilities, achieve high quality careers and helping employers hire and retain skilled workers. Title IV of *WIOA* amended title I of the *Rehabilitation Act of 1973*.

The State Rehabilitation Council is mandated in Section 105 of the Rehabilitation Act. It mandates a VR/SRC Partnership & provides the framework for the SRC voice.

Legislative Progression

WIOA

(Workforce Innovation & Opportunity Act)

Title IV of WIOA

(Rehabilitation Act)

Title I of Title IV

(VR Services)

Section 105 of Title I

(State Rehabilitation Council- SRC)

CFR 361.16 & 361.17

(SRC Implementing Regulations)

To have an informed voice, SRC members need a working understanding of the Rehabilitation Act, as amended in 2014, and they need an in-depth understanding of Section 105 of the Act and Sections 361.16 & 361.17 of the Regulations so that they:

→ feel comfortable entering into discussions concerning policy, procedures, long and short-range agency planning; &

→ have a basis for WIOA related discussions.

SRC duties focus on Title I of the Rehab Act- VR Services

- Declaration of policy, authorizations, & appropriations
- VR Services Portion of the Unified State Plan
- Eligibility & Individualized Plan for Employment
- VR Services
- State Rehabilitation Council
- Evaluation standards & performance indicators

- Monitoring & review
- Training & Services for Employers
- Client Assistance Program (CAP)
- Pre-employment transition services.
- American Indian VR services

SRC Composition, Appointments and Removals

Excerpt 2014 Amendment to Rehabilitation Act of 1973.

The full Act may be found in Title IV of the Workforce Investment & Opportunities Act of 1998.

Sec. 105. State Rehabilitation Council

§ 361.17 Requirements for a State Rehabilitation Council.
If the State has established a Council under § 361.16(a)(2) or (b), the Council must meet the following requirements:

(a) *Appointments -*

(1) The members of the Council must be appointed by the Governor or, in the case of a State that, under State law, vests authority for the administration of the activities carried out under this part in an entity other than the Governor (such as one or more houses of the State legislature or an independent board), the chief officer of that entity.

(2) The appointing authority must select members of the Council after soliciting recommendations from representatives of organizations representing a broad range of individuals with disabilities and organizations interested in individuals with disabilities. In selecting members, the appointing authority must consider, to the greatest extent practicable, the extent to which minority populations are represented on the Council.

(b) *Composition -*

(1) *General.* Except as provided in paragraph (b)(3) of this section, the Council must be composed of at least 15 members, including -

(i) At least one representative of the Statewide Independent Living Council, who must be the chairperson or other designee of the Statewide Independent Living Council;

(ii) At least one representative of a parent training and information center established pursuant to section 682(a) of the Individuals with Disabilities Education Act;

(iii) At least one representative of the Client Assistance Program established under part 370 of this chapter, who must be the director of or other individual recommended by the Client Assistance Program;

(iv) At least one qualified vocational rehabilitation counselor with knowledge of and experience with vocational rehabilitation programs who serves as an ex officio, nonvoting member of the Council if employed by the designated State agency;

(v) At least one representative of community rehabilitation program service providers;

(vi) Four representatives of business, industry, and labor;

(vii) Representatives of disability groups that include a cross section of -

(A) Individuals with physical, cognitive, sensory, and mental disabilities; and

(B) Representatives of individuals with disabilities who have difficulty representing themselves or are unable due to their disabilities to represent themselves;

(viii) Current or former applicants for, or recipients of, vocational rehabilitation services;

(ix) In a State in which one or more projects are funded under section 121 of the Act (American Indian Vocational Rehabilitation Services), at least one representative of the directors of the projects in such State;

(x) At least one representative of the State educational agency responsible for the public education of students with disabilities who are eligible to receive services under this part and part B of the Individuals with Disabilities Education Act;

(xi) At least one representative of the State workforce development board; and

(xii) The director of the designated State unit as an ex officio, nonvoting member of the Council.

(2) *Employees of the designated State agency.* Employees of the designated State agency may serve only as nonvoting members of the Council. This provision does not apply to the representative appointed pursuant to paragraph (b)(1)(iii) of this section.

(3) *Composition of a separate Council for a separate State agency for individuals who are blind.* Except as provided in paragraph (b)(4) of this section, if the State establishes a separate Council for a separate State agency for individuals who are blind, that Council must -

(i) Conform with all of the composition requirements for a Council under paragraph (b)(1) of this section, except the requirements in paragraph (b)(1)(vii), unless the exception in paragraph (b)(4) of this section applies; and

(ii) Include -

(A) At least one representative of a disability advocacy group representing individuals who are blind; and

(B) At least one representative of an individual who is blind, has multiple disabilities, and has difficulty representing himself or herself or is unable due to disabilities to represent himself or herself.

(4) *Exception.* If State law in effect on October 29, 1992 requires a separate Council under paragraph (b)(3) of this section to have fewer than 15 members, the separate Council is in compliance with the composition requirements in paragraphs (b)(1)(vi) and (viii) of this section if it includes at least one representative who meets the requirements for each of those paragraphs.

(c) *Majority -*

(1) A majority of the Council members must be individuals with disabilities who meet the requirements of § 361.5(c)(28) and are not employed by the designated State unit.

(2) In the case of a separate Council established under § 361.16(b), a majority of the Council members must be individuals who are blind and are not employed by the designated State unit.

(d) *Chairperson -*

(1) The chairperson must be selected by the members of the Council from among the voting members of the Council, subject to the veto power of the Governor; or

(2) In States in which the Governor does not have veto power pursuant to State law, the appointing authority described in paragraph (a)(1) of this section must designate a member of the Council to serve as the chairperson of the Council or must require the Council to designate a member to serve as chairperson.

(e) *Terms of appointment -*

(1) Each member of the Council must be appointed for a term of no more than three years, and each member of the Council, other than a representative identified in paragraph (b)(1)(iii) or (ix) of this section, may serve for no more than two consecutive full terms.

(2) A member appointed to fill a vacancy occurring prior to the end of the term for which the predecessor was appointed must be appointed for the remainder of the predecessor's term.

(3) The terms of service of the members initially appointed must be, as specified by the appointing authority as described in paragraph (a)(1) of this section, for varied numbers of years to ensure that terms expire on a staggered basis.

(f) *Vacancies -*

(1) A vacancy in the membership of the Council must be filled in the same manner as the original appointment, except the appointing authority as described in paragraph (a)(1) of this section may delegate the authority to fill that vacancy to the remaining members of the Council after making the original appointment.

(2) No vacancy affects the power of the remaining members to execute the duties of the Council.

(g) *Conflict of interest -*

No member of the Council may cast a vote on any matter that would provide direct financial benefit to the member or the member's organization or otherwise give the appearance of a conflict of interest under State law.

(h) *Functions –*

The Council must, after consulting with the State workforce development board -

(1) Review, analyze, and advise the designated State unit regarding the performance of the State unit's responsibilities under this part, particularly responsibilities related to -

(i) Eligibility, including order of selection;

(ii) The extent, scope, and effectiveness of services provided; and

(iii) Functions performed by State agencies that affect or potentially affect the ability of individuals with disabilities in achieving employment outcomes under this part;

(2) In partnership with the designated State unit -

(i) Develop, agree to, and review State goals and priorities in accordance with § 361.29(c); and

(ii) Evaluate the effectiveness of the vocational rehabilitation program and submit reports of progress to the Secretary in accordance with § 361.29(e);

(3) Advise the designated State agency and the designated State unit regarding activities carried out under this part and assist in the preparation of the vocational rehabilitation services portion of the Unified or Combined State Plan and amendments to the plan, applications, reports, needs assessments, and evaluations required by this part;

(4) To the extent feasible, conduct a review and analysis of the effectiveness of, and consumer satisfaction with -

(i) The functions performed by the designated State agency;

(ii) The vocational rehabilitation services provided by State agencies and other public and private entities responsible for providing vocational rehabilitation services to individuals with disabilities under the Act; and

(iii) The employment outcomes achieved by eligible individuals receiving services under this part, including the availability of health and other employment benefits in connection with those employment outcomes;

(5) Prepare and submit to the Governor and to the Secretary no later than 90 days after the end of the Federal fiscal year an annual report on the status of vocational rehabilitation programs operated within the State and make the report available to the public through appropriate modes of communication;

(6) To avoid duplication of efforts and enhance the number of individuals served, coordinate activities with the activities of other councils within the State, including the Statewide Independent Living Council established under chapter 1, title VII of the Act, the advisory panel established under section 612(a)(21) of the Individuals with Disabilities Education Act, the State Developmental Disabilities Planning Council described in section 124 of the Developmental Disabilities Assistance and Bill of Rights Act, the State mental health planning council established under section 1914(a) of the Public Health Service Act, and the State workforce development board, and with the activities of entities carrying out programs under the Assistive Technology Act of 1998;

(7) Provide for coordination and the establishment of working relationships between the designated State agency and the Statewide Independent Living Council and centers for independent living within the State; and

(8) Perform other comparable functions, consistent with the purpose of this part, as the Council determines to be appropriate, that are comparable to the other functions performed by the Council.

(i) *Resources -*

(1) The Council, in conjunction with the designated State unit, must prepare a plan for the provision of resources, including staff and other personnel, that may be necessary and sufficient for the Council to carry out its functions under this part.

(2) The resource plan must, to the maximum extent possible, rely on the use of resources in existence during the period of implementation of the plan.

(3) Any disagreements between the designated State unit and the Council regarding the amount of resources necessary to carry out the functions of the Council must be resolved by the Governor, consistent with paragraphs (i)(1) and (2) of this section.

(4) The Council must, consistent with State law, supervise and evaluate the staff and personnel that are necessary to carry out its functions.

(5) Those staff and personnel that are assisting the Council in carrying out its functions may not be assigned duties by the designated State unit or any other agency or office of the State that would create a conflict of interest.

(j) *Meetings –*

The Council must -

(1) Convene at least four meetings a year in locations determined by the Council to be necessary to conduct Council business. The meetings must be publicly announced, open, and accessible to the general public, including individuals with disabilities, unless there is a valid reason for an executive session; and

(2) Conduct forums or hearings, as appropriate, that are publicly announced, open, and accessible to the public, including individuals with disabilities.

(k) *Compensation –*

Funds appropriated under title I of the Act, except funds to carry out sections 112 and 121 of the Act, may be used to compensate and reimburse the expenses of Council members in accordance with section 105(g) of the Act.

The Council may use funds appropriated under this title to reimburse members of the Council for reasonable and necessary expenses of attending Council meetings and performing Council duties (including child care and personal assistance services), and to pay compensation to a member of the

Council, if such member is not employed or must forfeit wages from other employment, for each day the member is engaged in performing the duties of the Council.

(I) *Hearings and Forums –*

The Council is authorized to hold such hearings and forums as the Council may determine to be necessary to carry out the duties of the Council.

Relationship with the Governor's Office

SRCs are encouraged to develop a strong relationship with the key liaison in the Governor's Office who oversees appointments and can facilitate the appointment process. Meeting face-to-face is important so this person will know who you are. Work with them, ask when their busy times are and how you can help them get their job done to expedite the appointment process for your state or territory.

Be efficient submitting the completed paperwork in a timely manner and making sure your term limits mirror those of the Governor's Office. Educate the liaison on what your Council's requirements are and that the VR agency must comply to insure federal funding. Let them know that you appreciate their efforts and thank them on a regular basis. The more amicable your relationship and efficiency of the submitted paperwork, the better opportunities for swifter appointments.

The Governor generally appoints all SRC members. Anyone may nominate a person for membership on the SRC, if the person meets one of the mandated areas required for appointment. An advantage of establishing a good relationship with the Governor's staff is that this helps safeguard the Governor's confidence in the SRC recommendations for nominations.

Typically, SRCs will recruit, may interview, and approve nominees through the Membership Committee and consensus of the Council membership prior to the names being sent to the Governor for appointment. The Membership Committee will discuss the potential members to assure the state or territory meets the mandated composition required, is geographically composed, and people with differing abilities and ethnic backgrounds are represented to ensure diversity. The Governor's staff needs to be reassured that the nominated individuals will meet the requirements of the federal law and reflect positively on the Governor. All SRC members must be appointed by the Governor or appointing authority, including ex-officio, non-voting members.

Terms of Appointment

The law states that each member of the Council may serve for a term of three (3) years. A member may serve no more than two (2) full terms consecutively. A member appointed to complete someone else's unexpired term serves the remaining portion of that appointed term and must be appointed by the Governor. Once that term is complete, the newly appointed member is then eligible to request to serve another three (3) year term on the Council.

Term limits apply to voting members. Councils should strive so that appointments are staggered with experienced and inexperienced members on the Council. A member who has completed two (2) complete terms must comply with their state or territory's bylaws before applying to be considered for Council membership again.

Finally, the *majority* of the members (51%) must be people with disabilities who are not employed by a state agency. Some who cannot be included in the majority are:

☐ State agency representatives; and

☐ State employees who are not representing their agency, but are voting members.

Recruiting New Members

When seeking new members or reappointing members currently serving on the Council, be sure to look at the categories that the SRC must fulfill in order to be following & complying with the Federal law. Making sure you have chosen members wisely is vital to the success of your Council. Select individuals that will work as a team and contribute to your mission and vision.

Councils should interview prospective new members to make sure they understand the purpose of the SRC, the responsibilities and will have the time needed to be a collaborator and contributor. Ask potential members to complete a membership application, as well as any other document(s) required by your state or territory.

As a courtesy, prospective and re-appointments should be discussed with your VR director. Many states or territories require the SRC nominations go through the agency and their department before going to the Governor's office. This is another opportunity to have open communication with the agency.

Once names have been submitted to the Governor's Office, be sure to follow up with the Governor's liaison to assure the appointment process moves forward expeditiously.

New Member Orientation

Upon receiving notification that new members have been appointed, schedule an orientation for those members prior to them attending their first meeting. New members, especially those who have never previously served on the SRC, need education. Here are some suggestions on what you can do to help members understand the VR process and their role.

During this orientation refer to the 2019 rewrite of the 2011 36th IRI book "The State Rehabilitation Council – Vocational Rehabilitation Partnership" and cover those contents noted in the book. Developing an informational tabbed 3 ring notebook that members can store pertinent Council information at their fingertips, such as Bylaws, meeting schedules, minutes from meetings, Executive Director reports (if appropriate), financial statements, etc. is beneficial. This book can be found on the National Coalition of State Rehabilitation Councils, Inc. (NCSRC) website at www.ncsrc.net.

Bringing VR staff into the orientation so members can meet key players, allow VR staff time to discuss their role, the information they will be providing at meetings, the significance of why members need the data and what should be done with the materials disseminated is essential. This will help in having a full partnership with the agency and open communication.

Be sure to include a section in the notebook on acronyms and VR terminology (such as order of selection, needs assessment, WIOA, and state plan to name a few.) Encourage members to speak up and ask when terminology or data is used that they are not clear on the meaning or significance. For individuals who have never worked in the VR field, the terminology is confusing and can hamper members in their understanding of what is being discussed.

SRC Governance and Leadership

Council Bylaws

Bylaws are one of the most important legal documents that dictate how your SRC is governed. Bylaws are the written rules governing and setting forth the structure for an organization or corporation. Bylaws serve as a blueprint, along with policies and procedures, establish rights, determine day-to-day rules, provide comprehensive guidance to ensure effective operations, and may protect you when problems arise. Bylaws can direct and clarify SRC procedures, actions, and organizational structure. Bylaws may specify the qualifications, rights, and liabilities of membership, and the powers, duties, and grounds for dissolution of the organization.

Bylaws should not be confused with Articles of Incorporation, which state only the basic outline of the corporation. Bylaws generally provide for ~

☐ Establishing rules for conducting meetings;

☐ Electing officers or a board of directors;

☐ Filling vacancies & recommending removal when warranted after repeated unexcused absences;

☐ Posting notices and other open meetings as required by state law;

☐ Outlining types and duties of officers and committees; and

☐ Guiding the board in conducting business.

Bylaws are legal documents and must be formally adopted and/or amended. Carefully crafted bylaws, and adherence to them, can help ensure fairness of decisions and provide protection against legal challenges. Legal requirements for what should be included in bylaws vary depending on the state or territory in which you operate. To be sure your bylaws comply with the laws, you may want to consult an attorney before developing bylaws. *And be sure you follow your bylaws because they are legally binding.*

Council Policies or Handbook

Policies are clear, simple statements of how your SRC intends to operate and conduct business. They provide a set of guiding principles to help with decision making and consistency. They include principles, rules, and guidelines adopted for day-to-day tasks, conducting business, and reaching long-term goals. Written policies should cover board/council duties, personnel, and fiscal operations and should be approved by the SRC in an open meeting.

All staff and council members should read and have a written copy of the bylaws, as well as the policies and procedures. Each person should understand that they are expected to know and adhere to what those documents say. Policies and procedures should, at a minimum, include a code of ethics and standards of professional conduct and a conflict of interest policy and process that employees and council members should read and sign at the onset of their appointments.

Removal of Officers

Include procedures for removal of officers in the SRS's bylaws and policies to protect the SRC if the need arises. Some SRCs specify in their policies and procedures that any elected officer may be removed from office either with or without cause by a two-thirds (2/3) majority council vote. Policies may also state that "removal of officers may occur whenever in its judgment the interests of the SRC are best served. Furthermore, any such removal shall be without prejudice to the contract rights [will not affect contract rights], if any, of the officer so removed."

Resignation of Officers and Members

Bylaws and polices also need to cover the resignation of officers and members. Some SRC policies state that any elected officer or member may resign at any time by giving written notice to the council. Other policies require that notice be given to the Governor, with copies to the SRC chair and the Executive Director, if this applies to your Council.

Policies must also address the process for replacing officers who have been removed or have resigned.

Termination of SRC Staff

SRC policies should specifically describe when and how the executive director/administrator/coordinator can be terminated or removed. Some SRC policies state that the executive director, administrator, or coordinator can be terminated with or without cause by a two-thirds (2/3) majority council vote. Some SRC policies list reasons for termination while others are less specific and more general. Either way may be justified, if procedures and reasons for termination are covered in policies, preferably listed as with or without cause. Specific reasons may include:

☐ Failure to perform duties and follow policies and procedures;

☐ Substance abuse while working;

☐ Dishonesty; and/or

☐ Theft or damage to SRC property.

When termination occurs, consider providing the person the chance to resign first, if the reason for termination is not unlawful conduct.

If the staff person is an employee of the State, the SRC Executive Committee should meet with the VR Director to discuss the issues in order to comply with the agency's employment policies.

Example Standards

As stated, policies and procedures should include a code of ethics and standards of professional conduct and address full compliance with the established standards and ethics. Standards could include:

☐ Acting professionally, competently and honorably;

☐ Fulfilling assigned duties;

☐ Complying with standards established in performance appraisals;

☐ Maintaining an acceptable level of performance and conduct on all verbal and written job duties;

☐ Using funds prudently; and/or

☐ Reporting conditions and circumstances that may prevent the employee from performing their job effectively and safely.

Many SRCs also list examples of unacceptable conduct in their policies and procedures that violate policy and may result in disciplinary action, including immediate termination. Be sure your policies regarding terminating employees are within compliance of your state/territory law. Identifying every type of unacceptable conduct would be impossible; however, some examples might may be useful to craft your Council's policies are:

Examples of Unacceptable Conduct

☐ Refusal to follow instructions of the established authority or comply with a reasonable work request.

☐ Inefficient, careless, or unsatisfactory job performance.

☐ Neglect or abandonment of duties.

☐ Failure to get along, cooperate, or work harmoniously with council members, co-workers, vendors, or the public.

☐ Damaging, wasting, destroying, abusing, stealing, misappropriating, or unauthorized use of property, funds, equipment, or supplies.

☐ Failing to abide by occupational health and safety guidelines.

☐ Violating policies regarding discrimination and sexual harassment or other forms of harassment.

☐ Falsification or making material omissions on employment applications, time records, or other documents or records.

☐ Conducting personal business on SRC time.

☐ Giving or taking bribes or kickbacks in connection with SRC business.

☐ Engaging in business or activities that constitute a conflict of interest.

☐ Abuse of sick, vacation, holiday, family, and medical leave.

☐ Engaging in immoral or indecent conduct in the workplace or while representing the SRC in any capacity.

☐ Engaging in the use, possession, or distribution of sexually oriented or indecent materials.

☐ Excessive tardiness or absences from work.

☐ Reporting for duty while under the influence of alcohol or controlled substances.

☐ Bullying of Council members, agency staff or other partners.

☐ Downloading non work-related software or applications from the Internet.

☐ Offensive and abusive language.

Conflicts of Interest

Identify in the SRC's policies, procedures, and the code of ethics what a conflict of interest is and how this will be addressed. Conflicts of interest may occur when a council member or employee is in a position to influence a SRC decision that would result in personal or financial gain for themselves or a relative. All council members and employees should read and sign the conflict of interest policy and code of ethics, either annually or at the first meeting of their term(s).

> ➤ Council members and employees should have no personal agenda with the VR agency.

> ➤ Council members and employees should avoid any activity, investment, or association that might interfere or conflict with their judgment or duties.

> ➤ Conflicts of interest must be disclosed as soon as possible.

> ➤ Members should immediately disqualify themselves prior to discussion or voting on any matters where there is a conflict of interest.

> ➤ The policies and code of ethics should state that members must reveal the conflict as soon as possible and refrain from voting, discussing, or making decisions related to the conflict.

Voting

Voting procedures should be included in your bylaws, as well as your policies and procedures. Some SRCs require a two-thirds (2/3) majority vote and at least one member of the Executive Committee present, while others may require a simple majority, if there is a quorum present. A quorum should be defined in the bylaws and policies of your Council. This may be one more than fifty percent of members or a certain number of members with at least one member of the Executive Committee present.

Voting in person is recommended, but not always possible if a vote on something is needed right away. Taking action on an issue and voting when council members are spread across the state may be difficult. When votes are required in between meetings and sometimes during meetings, SRCs may turn to email; however, to ensure that votes taken by phone or email will hold up in court if challenged, SRCs should know what their state/territory laws require. Voting on actions by phone or email may or may not be legally binding, depending on the state/territory. There are currently six states (Alaska, Arkansas, Kentucky, Massachusetts, New Hampshire, and Oklahoma) with state statutes that do not address electronic voting.

In these states, SRC bylaws should determine voting procedures. SRCs may need to review a research report compiled on U.S. Laws governing nonprofit boards and electronic voting in 2012. This report contains a summary report, by state, of U.S. state laws on electronic voting by nonprofit boards. Legal codes, nonprofit legal information, state nonprofit associations and authorities regulating charities are also included in the report.

To access information and resources for your state, please visit http://boardeffect.com/wp-content/uploads/2015/01/Electronic-Voting-Report-FINAL.pdf.

Most other states/territories provide that board actions be taken at a meeting or by unanimous consent. A meeting does not always have to be in person. Definitions vary by state. Some other states require only majority written consent. A court could potentially overturn a vote made by email without signatures if someone objects. The reasoning is that there is a possibility that another person, not the council member, could send an email. If this is the case in your state, a proposed motion can be emailed, faxed or mailed to each council member, then signed, scanned, and emailed, faxed, or mailed back. Councils are advised to check on what your state/territory law requires to ensure that your voting procedures are in legal compliance.

The SRC has the responsibility to assure that all members have access to the information related to the item up for vote, that they are able to participate in the discussion, and that they are able to vote. More general information can be found at:

http://www.americanbar.org/publications/blt/2014/06/06_chatinover.html or http://www.blueavocado.org/content/can-nonprofit-boards-vote-email

Facilitating a Smooth-Running SRC

How to Chair, Guide, and Conduct a Meeting.

What makes for an effective meeting? Having a purpose, preparing ahead of time, setting goals during the meeting, and making provisions for follow-through afterwards. Plan carefully and develop an informative agenda.

There are three elements to your agenda ~ standard items like the introductions, having your mission statement visible, reserving time for anyone wishing to speak at the meeting or to review comments from the public at prior meetings, minutes from the last meeting, committee reports, financial statements; continuing old business from prior meetings that has not been resolved; and discussing any new business. Including presentations by agency staff to educate Council members is strongly recommended.

Members should receive the meeting agenda several days prior to the meeting. Some state statues also dictate dates for publishing agendas for public transparency.

Selection and Role of the Chairperson

The chairperson is selected by nomination from SRC membership by the voting
members. The chairperson or a designee is responsible for convening and presiding at all council and executive committee meetings.

The chairperson also ~

☐ Serves as a liaison to other agencies and entities.

☐ Performs as the SRC spokesperson, in partnership with the Executive Director or Chairperson of another SRC within the VR agency, if that position exists.

☐ Chairperson is responsible for conducting SRC business meetings.

☐ Establishes a working rapport with the Agency Director and their support staff.

☐ Appoints members to SRC committees.

☐ Oversees and coordinates the work of committees, task forces, or work teams.

☐ Conducts other duties specified in bylaws or otherwise designated by the SRC.

☐ Consults with the SRC Executive Director on staff activities, meeting agendas and obligations of the Council.

Tips for Chairpersons

A chairperson is organized.

☐ Think about what your goals are and what you would like (or need) to achieve from the council meeting;

☐ Review the draft agenda with appropriate council officers and staff;

☐ Revise the agenda as needed, then stick to it;

☐ Schedule time for everyone to introduce themselves, who they represent and geographic area where they live and work. This should also include guests;

☐ Allow time for discussion and opportunities for members to express new ideas. Provide a designated time at the beginning of all meetings for an "open forum" to allow the public to address the council and ensure that advance public notice is announced;

☐ Estimate how much time each item will take, to make sure that you will be able to move through the agenda and finish the meeting on time. You may even want to print this estimated time on your agenda to keep things moving; and,

☐ Send out information in advance (and provide alternate formats requested) if materials need to be reviewed, preferably at least one week prior to discussion, to guarantee access.

A chairperson orchestrates the meeting and keeps it moving.

☐ Encourage all members to participate and contribute to discussions. Make sure that all members feel welcome and know that all ideas will be considered;

☐ Sometimes members are not sure how to contribute. Some members may stay silent, making it difficult to move on without feedback or information. Find ways to draw them out. Ask for their comments directly. Try asking everyone on the council to state their opinion on certain issues. You can also ask if anyone feels differently when an opinion is expressed;

☐ Ask members if there is anything that will make them feel more comfortable or if they need anything else to fully participate;

☐ Break up into small groups or committees to discuss issues and make recommendations to the full council, especially when dealing with complex or difficult issues;

☐ Delegate tasks and make assignments so that the work is shared and progress is made;

☐ Make an effort to learn what the skills and limitations of your individual council members are. Put your members' skills and abilities to the best use to get tasks done effectively;

☐ Encourage members to work with each other so that they can learn new skills; and,

☐ Keep people moving towards the final goal.

Reminding the council to work as a team towards common goals and a mutual purpose may be necessary, but at the same time, respecting differences of opinion. Ask people to share their ideas, but not insist that their idea be the one decided on. *Members need to concede to the will of the majority.*

Sometimes one or two people try to monopolize the meeting. If this occurs, redirect back to the issue, or say that you would like to hear from everyone.

Ask that one topic at a time be considered. If a member states that an idea will not work, ask them what they think will.

During "open forum," if guests are critical and identify problems ask them to suggest solutions. Open forum with comments from the public should be for a set amount of time (usually 5 or 10 minutes) and then you should move to the next item on the agenda. **The council does not need to discuss or act on the comments during that meeting, and, in fact usually cannot act on an item that was not on the agenda due to open meetings laws (which vary by state).**

If an individual wants a longer period to address the council, ask them to submit a request, including how much time they need, and then place them on the agenda for the next meeting – also for a set amount of time. A council member can also ask that the item be added to the next meeting's agenda.

Try to always finish on time. People usually quit paying attention and become restless when the time to adjourn has passed. Others may need to leave if the meeting lasts more than a few minutes longer than planned.
Prepare the minutes so that they are not burdensome and do not include every detail, but still accurately reflect decisions. Minutes provide an outline or summary of the meeting with the location and start and ending time, names of attendees and those absent (excused and unexcused), the result of votes, decisions, and motions, and action items. Include who was assigned to complete each action item and when this is due. These action items can then be carried on your agenda as old or continuing business until they are complete.

Develop and use a template for meetings. The agenda is usually a good way to organize the minutes. Write in the same tense throughout the document. Most discussions need not be included in depth and just briefly summarized, if relevant. Ask someone else to review the minutes before they are distributed. Disseminate the agenda, minutes of the previous meeting, financial reports and any other handouts by email or mailing one (1) week prior to the scheduled Council meeting.

If more information is needed on how to chair a meeting, the American Federation of State, County and Municipal Employees has developed the following basic publication:

http://www.afscme.org/news-publications/publications/afscme-governance/pdf/How_to_Chair.pdf.

Robert's Rules of Order

These commonly used, time-tested rules provide procedures for conduct at council and board meetings. Information on Robert's Rules should be included in the council training, at least a written summary version, for those new members who are not familiar with procedures.

Guiding principles include the following:

☐ All members have a right to speak and to know what is going on at all times.

☐ Only one motion or issue may be discussed at a time and only urgent issues may interrupt someone who is speaking.

☐ A speaker may only be interrupted to get information about issues, rules, safety or comfort, and to appeal rulings.

Robert's Rules also specify how members express themselves.
☐ A motion is an idea, topic, proposal, or proposition that the entire council can take action on. Any member can introduce a motion, after being recognized by the chair of the council, when no other motion is being considered. Often a committee report takes the form of a motion for consideration.

☐ A second is required in order to discuss or consider the motion.

☐ Voting on motions usually requires a simple majority.

☐ A member who wishes to speak should indicate to the chair and wait to be recognized. Once recognized, the member should speak to the topic or the motion at hand.

☐ Wait to bring up new topics at the appropriate time, during the discussion/question period or when new business is being discussed.

Order of business:

☐ Call to order by the chair or presiding officer, which starts the meeting, once a quorum of members, as defined in the SRC bylaws, has been attained.

☐ Roll call.

☐ Public comments. Make sure guests are aware that comments should only be made during this designated time period, unless called upon by the membership.

☐ Reading the minutes of the last meeting and asking for any corrections.

☐ Approval of the minutes after corrections are finished and a motion is made.

☐ Review of financial statements and approval of statements by the council.

☐ Officer and committee reports.

☐ Special orders of business, continuing business, new business, and announcements.

☐ Adjournment.

Rules for Adjournment:

> ➤ A meeting is not adjourned until the chair declares it adjourned.
> ➤ There are two ways to reach the point of adjournment. When a member makes a motion to adjourn, a second may be made but is not needed, and then a majority vote to adjourn is required.
>
> ➤ A motion to adjourn is not debatable.
>
> ➤ The meeting may also be adjourned if the chair or presiding officer says "without objection the meeting is adjourned" and then waits to ensure there are no objections.
>
> ➤ If there are objections, the chair must continue the meeting unless a member makes a motion to adjourn.

Summary:

Robert's Rules should not be used to intimidate members or to manipulate the meeting to push through a personal agenda. Rather, Robert's Rules should be used to facilitate the process and ensure full discussion and deliberation of business and decision making.

Although Robert's Rules are quite detailed, a simplified summary can be found at:

https://blogs.cornell.edu/deanoffaculty/files/2016/01/RobertsRulesSimplified - 1ybt2mk.pdf and at:

http://diphi.web.unc.edu/files/2012/02/MSGROBERTS_RULES_CHEAT_SHEET.pdf

Dealing with Conflict

Bear in mind that "rubber stamp" councils are not as functional or useful as those with members who express strong opinions and consider issues from a variety of viewpoints. However, if council meetings are highly emotional or conflictual, consider strategies to help the meetings run more smoothly.

☐ When emotions are running high, take a break and let things cool down.

☐ After everyone returns, start by discussing the shared purpose of helping people with disabilities live more independently, the SRC goals, and/or the specific goal of the task at hand.

☐ Ask members not to think about winning or losing their arguments, but to focus on maintaining good council relationships and being effective.

☐ Let members explain why they prefer their ideas or methods. If the council is going in circles, ask everyone to brainstorm new or different approaches that might work and try to think outside the box. If there is still disagreement, form a committee or work group to examine the ideas in more depth, present pros and cons, and recommend the two best solutions to the council.

Just one council member may create conflict, derail discussions, hamper productive meetings, and decrease the work and success of your SRC. Challenging popular viewpoints can actually be a really good thing, but consistently being negative, ignoring confidentiality, bullying other members, disrupting meetings, and being disrespectful or destructive.

There are different strategies that can be considered when issues such as these arise:

☐ Whenever a person criticizes an idea or strategy, ask what they think would work better. You can also change the subject or ask for other opinions.

☐ If there is any type of bullying or abusive behavior, stop it immediately. Make sure that your policies include anti-bullying. Remind members that the council is committed to a safe and healthy, inclusive environment with a culture of respect for everyone.

☐ Try to remain calm and not take things personally.

Meeting with the member(s) creating the conflict one-on-one may help to better understand the person's perspective which may be helpful to identify and resolve the issue. Suggest other ways of communicating and addressing the concerns. Sometimes just asking what the problem is makes that member feel respected and heard and ultimately moves things along more constructively.

Council members who do not regularly attend meetings can also decrease morale and slow progress. This may be addressed by policies and a good relationship with your Governor's office. Some SRC policies state that members who miss a given number of meetings in one year without informing the chair or executive director of the reason for their absence will be submitted to the Governor's office for removal from the council.

If a person misses one meeting without a valid reason, the chair or staff should reach out and ask why they could not attend. You may consider allowing a leave of absence if the person is having a long-term medical or personal issue. If the person continues to miss meetings, and generally does not participate, a respectful way of termination may be to ask the person if he or she would like to be released from the council as it appears that their time does not allow full participation. You can ask if they would like you to draft a letter for their review and approval that confirms their resignation due to lack of time. The signed letter would then be forwarded to the governor with copies to the chair and executive director.

Setting Up Committees

Committees are vital as they essentially do most of the required SRC tasks. Their activities advance the goals of the SRC.   Most importantly, they typically develop and monitor the implementation of the State Plan. Committees greatly contribute to the overall functioning, efficiency, and productivity of the SRC.

Encourage all council members to serve on a committee. This will help new members learn and ensure that everyone contributes. Remind members that all committees are accountable and cannot operate independently. All committees are units of the SRC, doing work for and reporting to the SRC. The entire council must vote on any items presented by a committee before those items are approved and implemented.

There are several ways to set up committees. There is no specific number of committees or categories that are ideal, or a right or wrong way, just whatever works best for your SRC. Some SRCs have as few as three or four committees, while others operate with several more. Some of the SRCs with only four or five committees may include the following categories (combined):

- Executive, administrative or governance;

- Unified or Combined State Plan;

- Policy & Legislation;

- Annual Report;

- Consumer Satisfaction & Needs Assessment

The SRC's bylaws should describe the specific function and authority of the Executive Committee. You cannot utilize the executive committee to get around open meeting requirements in your state. Like any other committee, the Executive Committee must report to the full council. As allowed in your state, the Executive Committee may take on specific tasks on behalf of and at the request of the council, such as the evaluation of the SRC Executive Director, if your Council employees this person.

Additional committees SRCs may have could include public policy, bylaws, finance, membership or nominating, and any other pertinent committees. There are also ad hoc committees, which are formed for a specific task or purpose and then dissolved after that task is completed. A number of SRCs include volunteers, who are not part of the council, on specific committees. These volunteers typically enrich committees, providing needed expertise, knowledge, time, and energy. Dedicated volunteer committee members can be encouraged to apply for appointment to the SRC, if they are interested. At a minimum they become oriented and educated about the SRC through the committee work.

When first setting up and organizing committees, figure out the purpose, authority, and the scope of each committee. Standing committees should be included and described in SRC bylaws. Make sure that there is enough work to justify any separate committee(s).

Some SRCs believe smaller committees are more efficient, but that is an individual determination. Define the frequency of meetings, with additional meetings added as necessary. Ask members their personal interests or expertise and suggest their involvement on those committees. Determine who would excel on the committees, how many people should be on the committee, when the committee(s) should meet. Determine who the best person will be as the chair—preferably someone who is a leader with the ability to draw people out and work well with all members.

Ask the chairs to send out the agenda before the meeting, to start and end on time, present a written report of each meeting for the Council minutes to the Secretary, send committee members the minutes of the meetings, and report to the membership at the first meeting following the committee meeting. Annually ask for feedback from all committee members on how each committee is working. Provide committee members the opportunity to work on other committees when desired and appoint those with no preference to the committee where the chairperson feels the member could contribute most.

Keep in mind, committees do not necessarily need to meet every month, but as necessary to meet deadlines, this will help motivate members to participate.

Traits of a Good Council Member

Besides obtaining a working knowledge of the SRC, vocational rehabilitation and disability issues, what other qualities make a good council member?

☐ *Have a Commitment to Disability Rights*—To start with, it is best if you are committed to the rights of, and improving services for, people with disabilities and furthering the mission of the SRC in your state. Working or volunteering in the disability arena is not about the money. It is more about giving back to the community while working on improving social justice, independence, and quality of life for children and adults with disabilities within your state.

☐ **Bring Your Skills**—Bring the skills, experience, and connections you have to the work of the SRC. Your skills in finance, planning, public relations, writing, social media, etc. are valuable assets to the SRC. Offer your skills and connections to the council to maximize your membership and the SRC's effectiveness.

☐ **Learn New Skills**—In addition to learning new information, it is helpful if you are willing to learn new skills in financial management, strategic planning,
evaluation, etc. It takes time and effort to acquire knowledge and skills, but these abilities will benefit both your SRC and you personally.

☐ **Develop Relationships**—You should develop relationships and make friends with other SRC members and staff. It will make meetings and work groups more enjoyable and effective. Try to learn the names and responsibilities of the other council members and staff as soon as you can. Treat staff as equal partners.

☐ **Respect and Listen to Others**—It is helpful if you listen to others and consider different issues from all sides. Try to stay on good terms with everyone, even if someone opposes you. Respect confidences and privacy. Gather information if needed. Ask questions about anything that is confusing or that you need more information about. Other people most likely feel the same way.

☐ **Voice Your Opinion**—Voice your opinion, especially if you have different information or views. Your opinion counts and makes a difference. Try not to take it personally if people vote against something that you want. Consider a compromise when necessary to move ideas forward and help everyone feel that their opinions were heard.

☐ **Participate Fully**—Of course, making sure that you attend and actively participate in all council and committee meetings is the most basic, but nevertheless, important quality. Be on time. Make sure that you let the chair know if you are unavoidably late or cannot make a meeting. The willingness to serve on a work committee and take action where needed moves the work of the council forward. Councils need active, engaged members. Read agendas and attachments that are sent out ahead of time before you attend meetings.

☐ **Follow Through**—Do everything that you say you are going to do. If you run into difficulty completing a task, let the chair know and ask for help. If you fail to meet your obligations, other committee or council members will have to pick up the slack. If you come up with a new idea, be willing to help make that idea happen.

☐ **Remember the Big Picture**—Be proactive and attentive, but focus on the big important stuff, such as where the SRC and the Independent Living Network are going, how they are doing, and current strategies / policies, not minor details. Try to monitor what is happening to stay ahead of problems instead of reacting to a crisis.

☐ **Offer Solutions**—If you point out a concern, try not to blame or point fingers and always offer a solution. Things will move forward if criticism is constructive and includes possible solutions or steps to resolve the issue. On the other hand, make sure to show your appreciation for other members and the SRC staff. Many times, people will hear what is going wrong, or needs to be improved, but do not hear about the things that are going right or that they are doing well.

☐ **Be an Ambassador**—Share information about your SRC through social media and with the social and professional groups that you belong to. There is a section on social media later in this document.

Recruiting, Orientating & Training New Establishing Council Members

Recruiting New Council Members

Term limits result in an ongoing need to recruit new council members. High turnover, poor attendance, members with inadequate knowledge, or members who are uncomfortable with their responsibilities may also result in the need for recruitment of new council members. Recruiting can be challenging. Council composition is always changing. Sometimes, securing appointments takes a long time and potential new members lose interest. The SRC must recruit individuals who keep the council in compliance with the requirements in the law and its bylaws while ensuring diversity and necessary skills. Consider different approaches and adapt them to target and recruit the council members you need.

Planning and developing a strategy is important. Analyze where your gaps are. Think about the composition of an ideal well-balanced council. Enough people are needed to fulfill requirements and actually do the work, yet not so many that everything becomes a huge process without being able to move quickly and get things done.

As a reminder, qualifications include statewide representation and a broad range of people with disabilities from diverse backgrounds who are, or will become, knowledgeable about the SRC. A tracking spreadsheet can help ensure that your council is complying. This tool does not need to be too complicated. The spreadsheet may include geography, disabilities, race, ethnicity, etc., and agencies represented. You may also want to list age group to ensure youth representation and diversity of ages. One way to set the spreadsheet up is so pertinent areas automatically calculates disability majority percentage. That way, at any given moment, you can see if the council at a glance or who you need to recruit to be complying.

Consider which agencies (perhaps as ex-officio non-voting members), groups, and councils are mandated and who else the SRC needs to coordinate with to ensure effective services are provided for consumers. These agencies or programs might include Medicaid, housing, transportation, education, Veterans Administration, assistive technology programs, protection and advocacy, domestic violence shelters, area agencies on aging, and employers.

General recruitment can be conducted through delivery methods such as—

☐ Newsletters,
☐ Public service announcements/press releases,
☐ Newspapers,
☐ Email lists, and/or
☐ Flyers

Social media (Facebook, Twitter, LinkedIn, YouTube, Instagram, Pinterest, StumbleUpon, Blogs) can be effective, especially for recruiting youth. Personal recruitment is often the most effective. Try to make the process easy for your members, SRCs, VR and other partners to recruit. Some SRCs have developed a small fact card that can be carried in a wallet or purse. Other SRCs have added a page in their annual report that can be removed and sent to the SRC for consideration. An SRC could develop a recruitment tool that identifies current targets, describes where to look for recruits, and what to tell recruits about SRC membership.

Some places to look for potential members include —

☐ Partner and other disability organizations,
☐ Service agencies,
☐ State agency administrators,
☐ Forums or focus groups,
☐ Disability support groups,
☐ Conferences,
☐ Work groups,
☐ Friends of council members,
☐ Consumers from the CILs,
☐ Current or former board members of your SRCs, and
☐ Past SRC members who have been off the council, who might now be willing to be re-appointed.

Potential members can be invited to attend SRC meetings. They may learn answers to questions that they did not know they had. Individuals may serve as a volunteer on SRC committees before their names are put forward as nominees for appointment to the full council.

When you find a potential applicant, explain to them what the SRC does and estimate how much time is generally required. For those who look promising and are interested, send or hand them a recruitment packet. This packet could consist of:

☐ A recruitment flyer,
☐ List of responsibilities of SRC members,
☐ Position description for council members,
☐ SRC brochure,
☐ SRC application,
☐ Most recent SRC newsletter, if applicable,
☐ SRC annual report,
☐ Membership policies, and
☐ Mission & Vision statements

Keep a record of the applications that are given out. Follow-up with applicants after three or four weeks. Decide as a Council whose responsibility this is: the chair, the nominating committee chair, or the SRC staff. Have a committee or workgroup review all applications received, check references, and interview all interested candidates.

Sometimes an application may need to be held until a later date, due to balancing the council in terms of geography, disability, ethnicity, skills or the number of members currently serving. The committee/workgroup should present all names of the nominees to the full Council to be voted on prior to being submitted to the Governor for appointment. Some states may require the Council to submit nominee names to the VR agency who then submits to the Governor through their Department.

To expedite the appointment process, hand-delivering the information for appointments to the office or person assigned to handle such appointments in the Governor's office is recommended.

Remember, the nominee(s) are not SRC members until the Governor's appointment process is completed. Their expenses may not be covered until the official appointment letter has been received by the SRC. Ex-officio members, including the VR Director are exempt from the SRC's application and interview process, *but must be appointed by the governor and should not subject to term limits.*

Orientation and Training for New Members

Learning about the SRC, laws, regulations, the Designated State Agency, logistics, etc., can seem overwhelming. One person may know very little about the SRC, while someone else may be quite experienced. A person's understanding can be gauged by asking what they understand about a topic and how this may be described.

If possible, provide orientation and training for new members shortly before their first official council meeting after being appointed. Make sure that they are provided an acronym list, your handbook, minutes in electronic, print, or alternative format (as needed) for the last several meetings, financial reports, SRC staff reports, past annual reports, and a link to your website. Follow-up training may be done in person or by phone or web conference on a weekly, biweekly, semi-monthly, or monthly basis. Invite seasoned Council members to attend orientations as a refresher and to assist in helping new members gain more knowledge and meet fellow Council members.

Providing training quickly can help to minimize confusion at council meetings. No one likes to feel lost and overwhelmed. Make a consorted effort to take time on the front end whenever possible, before members attend the first meeting and are assigned responsibilities. Consider providing new members with peer mentors who are on the council. They do not need to live near one another, but mentors should be available by phone or email to answer occasional questions or concerns when they come up.

Questions are generally about the SRC philosophy but may be about anything. This can be reassuring to the new council member to know there is someone who can give clarification or assistance when needed. Better results may be obtained if both orientation and ongoing training are person centered and interactive. Although providing one-on-one or small group orientation and training takes more time, trainees are usually more engaged. They can talk, learn definitions of terms, ask questions, and not feel foolish. Encourage them to ask any question that comes to mind.

Some new members may feel intimidated and not understand the terminology, SRC structure, or their roles. Support them in building their confidence. One-on-one or small group sessions can help new members feel more confident and comfortable, which will contribute to increased participation.

Make sure that your policies and procedures include a discussion of unlawful harassment (unwelcome conduct based on race, color, gender, sexual orientation, religion, national origin, age [40 or older], disability, or genetic information). More on harassment can be found at the U.S. EEOC website at: https://www.eeoc.gov/laws/types/harassment.cfm.

Train in small doses, if possible. The SRC and VR programs can be complexed. There is a lot of information to absorb. This may be hard for new members to retain so many details if too much information is provided at once. After the initial training has occurred, ask questions to gauge their comprehension. Ask them what they understand or how they would describe the topic. Provide them with written materials that they can review.

An acronym list is a MUST! Provide all members with a list, as jargon can be very confusing to understand. Make sure the acronym list is updated and also on your website. Remind members if an acronym is used during a meeting and they are not familiar with the term, to speak up and ask what the acronym means. There are web sites that have terms available as a guide. Be sure to update and edit the acronym list to be specific to your state or territory.

All council members, SRC employees and agency liaisons should read and understand the bylaws, as well as the Council's policies and procedures. Have members sign a form indicating they have done so. Everyone should read and sign the conflict of interest policy and code of ethics as well. All SRC members
and employees need to understand that they are expected to know and adhere to these documents.

Suggested SRC orientation topics include:

☐ Understanding the relationship of the SRC and VR;
☐ Acronyms;
☐ Key players and partners;
☐ Laws and regulations;
☐ SRC activities;
☐ Unified or Combined State Plan;
☐ Consumer Satisfaction Surveys; and
☐ Their duties as a member.

There are also two (2) annual national conferences. One in the spring held in the Washington, D.C. area and the fall conference, which is announced on the Council of State Administrators of Vocational Rehabilitation (CSAVR) website www.csavr.org and includes the next following year locations. Some areas have regional SRC meetings.

During these national conferences, the SRCs have the opportunity for in depth training the weekend prior to the CSAVR conferences. The National Coalition of State Rehabilitation Councils (NCSRC) provide Councils guidance in every aspect of the roles and responsibilities of the Council. CSAVR is supportive in this learning mechanism to strengthen our roles and be a vital part of the broader picture. You are encouraged to discuss with your state agencies if there is the opportunity to attend the national trainings. There are also conference calls conducted on the second Tuesday of the even months that any Council member or agency liaison may participate.

Resource Development

Each state and territory will handle the resources of their SRC differently. Some Councils have a dedicated grant or contract with their state or territory. Others may be a line item in the agency budget.

For SRCs that are a grant or contract, the Council may manage their funds independently. The Council should receive a financial report at every meeting. SRCs may be required to submit financial reports to their respective agencies giving the agency an accounting of expenses. Councils may vary in how funding is disseminated.

Some states and territories grant the funds at the beginning of the fiscal year for the entire year while other will bill the agency on a monthly or quarterly basis. This should include having an audit or compilation report completed by an outside CPA consultant for checks and balances annually.

In other cases, the VR agency or a designated agency will manage the SRC funding, writing of checks and reporting will be specific to their policies. In these instances, the agency will require approval on expenditures, determine forms necessary for payment, complete the payments for all expenses incurred by the Council members and should provide the Council with a report on the Council budget status.

SRC Financial Management

All SRC staff should also understand basic financial management standards. Periodic training should also occur for all staff whose job is affected by financial policies and regulations.

The SRC needs to have financial policies and a policy manual. The council must establish and then update/revise the policies and procedures on a regular basis.

☐ Engage key staff and council members in the development process.

☐ Determine roles and responsibilities for committees, the council, the executive director, and accountant or bookkeeper in developing policies.

☐ Determine a process for review and approval, including final approval by the full council when necessary.

☐ Ensure that council minutes reflect the date of adoption of the policies and procedures and any revisions.

☐ Make sure that the date of adoption and any revisions are included on the financial policy manual. The dates should include the date of first adoption and all revisions, to show continual efforts are being made to ensure sound financial management.

☐ Establish when reviews will occur, such as on an annual basis.

☐ The policies and procedures should identify that the council reviews and approves the most recent financial statements (including a year-to-date comparison of budget to actual expenditures).

Transparency and Accountability Are Key

Financial management systems must be accurate, current, and fully disclosed. Financial management should ensure effective and efficient operations, reliable financial reporting, and regulatory compliance. There must be a clear paper trail that allows auditors and federal reviewers to follow money from its point of award to the receipt of cash, drawdowns, expenditures, and cash after expenses. Source documentation shows all expenses, justification of travel, activities and prior approvals by RSA, approval as required in procedures, proper allocation of shared or indirect costs, and the funding source.

Internal controls should include—

☐ Policies on how federal funds are safeguarded;

☐ Separation of duties for approving purchases, check signing, and appropriate checks and balances;

☐ Conflict of interest policy; and

☐ An independent audit or compilation report annually.

Conflict of interest means that a person may not make an administrative decision if they or their family directly benefit, if they are a public official, if they have a family or business relationship with the grantee, or if they are motivated by personal gain. The IRS Form 990 for nonprofit corporations asks for a written conflict of interest policy and procedures for identifying and dealing with conflicts of interest. Fiscal control and accounting procedures must ensure the proper disbursement of and accounting for federal funds.

Remember ~ Federal dollars cannot be used to lobby for more federal dollars, to influence federal officials, legislators, or Congress in connection with awarding federal funds or to influence legislation. Federal dollars cannot be used to make contributions to political parties or to form lobbying organizations.

Partnering with Other Organizations

The SRC should collaborate and coordinate with and encourage and support other disability organizations as well as agencies that may only occasionally serve children and adults with disabilities. There should be a strong working relationship with these organizations. Maximize these relationships in the way that you write your state plan.

Consider having SRC members and staff serve on other councils, commissions, advisory committees and boards. These may include ~

☐ Statewide Independent Living Council (SILC)
☐ Developmental Disabilities Council
☐ Protection and advocacy board and advisory committees
☐ The state assistive technology program council
☐ Social Security determination board
☐ Olmstead council
☐ Accessible housing boards or committees
☐ College disability resource centers
☐ Domestic violence shelter boards
☐ Aging services/Aging and Disability Resource Centers
☐ Recreation centers
☐ Transition service agencies
☐ Community action agencies
☐ Homeless coalitions
☐ School special education programs
☐ Family or parent centers
☐ Hospitals

☐ Governor's commission on disability

Forming relationships and serving on boards and committees can provide opportunities to collaborate with a lot of other partners and have an influence on the kinds of decisions that are being made. By being involved with other organizations, SRCs can make sure that people with disabilities are included and considered, this paves the way of doing systems advocacy.

Examples of Collaborating and Building Partnerships

Consumer Satisfaction

Collaboration is critical to effectively accomplishing tasks in many areas. SRCs should collaborate with their designated state agency to assess consumer satisfaction with VR functions, services and employment outcomes. This can be completed in a variety of ways.

States or territories may disseminate surveys in a variety of ways:

VR counselors may mail or give the client the survey
The agency may contract with an outside entity to conduct the survey
The SRC might solely perform this task

Preparing a formal report on the service areas for the agency and SRC is vital.
Some agencies survey all closed cases, while others may only use a percentage of the cases. How the data needed is gathered will be determined by the individual state or territory. This is a report card for service delivery and satisfaction and results should be discussed in a joint meeting with the pertinent agency staff and Council members. Regardless of whether the report if prepared by an independent consultant who receives the responses or a staff person, the outcomes are important to meeting the agency's requirements for RSA and knowing their successes and needs.

The person preparing the report should prepare a report that encompasses statewide comments and satisfactions marks for the agency that VR and SRCs use for planning and evaluating activities. If there are costs relating to the printing, mailing of surveys, and/or an independent consultant, those are normally handled by the agency, but may be included in the SRC budge, if the Council is responsible for this activity.

Participation in statewide conference and activities that provides training on leadership, self-advocacy, peer support, and disability rights laws are vital for the SRC. There are usually numerous of attendees, including consumers, family members, and advocates at these events. RSA had said that the these are a great way to get input and feedback from consumers, but there are limitations in how SRC funds can be used to support some of these functions. SRC may collaborate with their state agency, SILC, DD Council, Protection and Advocacy organization, University Center for Excellence on Developmental Disabilities, Olmstead Office, and many other organizations, foundations, and individuals to support the full cost of the caucus.

Mandated Functions in *Partnership* with VR

Review, analyze, & advice regarding responsibilities under the Act, particularly related to –

- ✧ Eligibility & Order of Selection
- ✧ Extent, Scope, & Effectiveness of Services
- ✧ Functions affecting individual achievement of employment outcomes
- ✧ Applications, reports, & evaluations.
- ✧ Develop, agree to, & review state goals & priorities.
- ✧ Evaluate effectiveness of VR program & submit progress reports to the Commissioner.

Advise & assist in the preparation of ~

- ➢ the State Plan portion of the Unified or Combined State Plan, & Amendments;
- ➢ the applications, reports, needs assessments, & evaluations.

Participate in Statewide Needs Assessment every 3-years. Focusing on:

- • Most significant disabilities
- • Minorities
- • Unserved & underserved
- • Served through Workforce Investment System
- • Students & Youths with Disabilities, including Pre-Employment Transition Services
- • Community Rehab Centers

Review & analyze the effectiveness of AND the consumer satisfaction with ~
- • VR services
- • VR services provided by other state agencies & other public & private entities
- • Employment outcomes achieved by eligible individuals (including availability of health & other employment benefits)

Prepare Annual Report on VR Program Status to submit to the Governor & Commissioner. This report is to be made available to the public.

Perform other functions that the ~

- SRC determines to be appropriate & consistent with the purpose of Title I (Subtitle B); and,
- Are comparable to other SRC mandated functions.

Agency Mandates regarding SRC in Title 1 should include:

- Jointly develop, agree to & review annually VR agency goals & priorities.
- Consult regularly re development, implementation, & revision of policies & procedures pertaining to VR services.
- Include summary of SRC input in State Plan.
- Jointly conduct statewide needs assessment every 3 years
- Gain SRC review & comment on CSPD.

The agency should be routinely transmitting copies of following to SRC:

- All plans, reports, & other information required to be submitted to RSA.
- All policies & information on practices & procedures provided to or used by rehab personnel in carrying out VR program.
- Due process hearing decisions transmitted to SRC in a manner to protect individual confidentiality.

WIOA <u>mandates</u> the SRC/VR partnership and voice throughout this process and your SRC Needs ~

☐ Annual targeted goals & action steps to accomplish SRC charges.
☐ Member commitment to time & work necessary to achieve the desired outcomes.

Understanding Sec. 121 Programs ~ American Indian Vocational Rehabilitation Services Program

The purpose of this program is to assist tribal governments to develop or to increase their capacity to provide a program of vocational rehabilitation services, in a culturally relevant manner, to American Indians with disabilities residing on or near federal or state reservations. The program's goal is to enable these individuals, consistent with their individual strengths, resources, priorities, concerns, abilities, capabilities, and informed choice, to prepare for and engage in gainful employment. Program services are provided under an individualized plan for employment and may include native healing services.

The program provides financial assistance for the establishment and operations of VR services programs for American Indians with disabilities living on or near a federal or state reservation. The state vocational programs can share in the cost of VR services for Native Americans in both VR programs.

Not all states or territories will have active 121 Programs and states with active programs may vary in number. States that have a 121 Program are required to have the Director or their designee participate as an SRC member. Best practices would allow an SRC to adopt in their own by-laws that each 121 Program be represented since each tribal VR program is different and each tribe is different.

Unified or Combined State Plan

Options for Submitting a State Plan

A State has two options for submitting a State Plan— a Unified State Plan or a Combined State Plan. At a minimum, a State must submit a Unified State Plan that meets the requirements described in this document and outlines a four-year strategy for the core programs. The six core programs are—

> o the Adult Program (Title I of WIOA),
> o the Dislocated Worker Program (Title I),
> o the Youth Program (Title I),
> o the Adult Education and Family Literacy Act Program (Title II), and
> o the Wagner-Peyser Act Program (Wagner-Peyser Act, as amended by title III),
> o the Vocational Rehabilitation Program (Title I of the Rehabilitation Act of 1973, as amended by Title IV).

Alternatively, a State may submit a Combined State Plan that meets the requirements described in this document and outlines a four-year strategy for WIOA's core programs plus one or more of the Combined State Plan partner programs. When a State includes a Combined State Plan partner program in their Combined State Plan, the state need not submit a separate plan or application for that particular program.

If included, Combined State Plan partner programs are subject to the "common planning elements" (Sections II and III of this document) where specified, as well as the program-specific requirements for that program. The Combined State Plan partner programs are—

o Career and technical education programs authorized under the Carl D. Perkins Career and Technical Education Act of 2006 (20 U.S.C. 2301 et seq.)

o Temporary Assistance for Needy Families Program (42 U.S.C. 601 et seq.)

o Employment and Training Programs under the Supplemental Nutrition Assistance Program (Programs authorized under section 6(d)(4) of the Food and Nutrition Act of 2008 (7 U.S.C. 2015(d)(4)

o Work programs authorized under section 6(o) of the Food and Nutrition Act of 2008 (7 U.S.C. 2015(o))
o Trade Adjustment Assistance for Workers Programs (Activities authorized under chapter 2 of title II of the Trade Act of 1974 (19 U.S.C. 2271 et seq.)

o Jobs for Veterans State Grants Program (Programs authorized under 38, U.S.C. 4100 et. seq.)

o Unemployment Insurance Programs (Programs authorized under State unemployment compensation laws in accordance with applicable Federal law)

o Senior Community Service Employment Program (Programs authorized under title V of the Older Americans Act of 1965 (42 U.S.C. 3056 et seq.)

o Employment and training activities carried out by the Department of Housing and Urban Development

o Community Services Block Grant (Employment and training activities carried out under the Community Services Block Grant Act (42 U.S.C. 9901 et seq.)

o Reintegration of Ex-Offenders Program (Programs authorized under section 212 of the Second Chance Act of 2007 (42 U.S.C. 17532))

How State Plan Requirements Are Organized

The major content areas of the Unified or Combined State Plan include strategic and operational planning elements. WIOA separates the strategic and operational elements to facilitate cross-program strategic planning.

> o The **Strategic Planning Elements** section includes analyses of the State's economic conditions, workforce characteristics, and workforce development activities. These analyses drive the required vision and goals for the State's workforce development system and alignment strategies for workforce development programs to support economic growth.

> o The **Operational Planning Elements** section identifies the State's efforts to support the State's strategic vision and goals as identified in the Strategic Planning Elements section. This section ensures that the State has the necessary infrastructure, policies, and activities to meet its strategic goals, implement its alignment strategy, and support ongoing program development and coordination. Operational planning elements include:

> • State Strategy Implementation,
> • State Operating Systems and Policies,
> • Assurances, and
> • Program-Specific Requirements for the Core Programs, and
> • Program-Specific Requirements for the Combined State Plan partner programs. (These requirements are available in a separate supplemental document, *Supplement to the Workforce and Innovation Act (WIOA) Unified and Combined State Plan Requirements*. The Departments are not seeking comments on these particular requirements).

When responding to Unified or Combined State Plan requirements, States must identify specific strategies for coordinating programs and services for target populations. While discussion of and strategies for every target population is not expected, States must address as many as are applicable to their State's population and look beyond strategies for the general population.

The Council should make recommendation to be included in the State Plan for Vocational Services. These recommendations are based on reports provided during regular Council meetings, memorandums and other communication offered by the agency director and/or the staff of the agency. These reports guarantee the Council is receiving factual updates and pertinent information to make accurate observations, decisions, policies and recommendations.

This task is taken very seriously by the Council knowing that the acceptance and monitoring of the State Plan assures the Federal government that states and territories will operate its vocational rehabilitation (VR) programs in accordance with the provisions of this Plan, as well as meeting federal statutory, regulatory and policy requirements.

Councils should be a supportive partner and advocate of VR. Councils maintain a diverse group of individuals comprised of representatives who represent many backgrounds, including the SILC, business, labor & industry, Client Assistant Program (CAP), Community Rehabilitation Programs (CRPs), other services providers, Vocational Rehabilitation counselors, Workforce Investment Board, Department of Education, consumers and consumer advocates. Value these partnerships, as well as the unique working relationship they bring to your membership.

Work toward establishing a strong bond with the SILC in your state or territory. These steadfast partnerships remain a vital core of our mission and vision allowing the Council more insight of consumer needs. Remember, you are working toward many of the same goals.

Sharing agency data regarding programs, services, policy, fiscal status or other pertinent issues is invaluable to the success of the agency and Council. Agencies can provide informative education when making presentations to your membership during each meeting, or as needed. Appreciate your agency liaisons to your Council, who are valuable assets, informed resources and contributors to your members. Some states have a non-voting Counselor Representative member which adds more expertise and voices for their peers in helping direct the SRCs.

Understand the agency's obligation in determining and achieving the benchmarks as set by RSA. Assure that all Council members have a clear understanding of expectations of the agency staff, what this means for the agency, sharing of statistics and allowing time for members to ask questions during their regularly scheduled presentations during your meetings. With the new changes in the law, make sure time is allocated to educate the Council members.

Endeavor to have open communication and continuous support with the agency director and their staff. The Council should strive to maintain this collaboration and embrace the opportunity to serve as a partner and trusted confidant of the agency.

Agencies will vary on how the information is gathered and should be forthcoming with information to the Council with this data.

Conducting the Needs Assessments

Start the needs assessment process early. Remember:

☐ All relevant stakeholders need to be fully committed for the needs assessment, data collection, and reporting to be successful.

☐ Obtaining input from individuals with disabilities and other stakeholders within the community is important for several reasons.

Keep in mind that Title I Programs, Vocational Rehabilitation, are required to conduct a Comprehensive Needs Assessment Survey. Leverage your VR agency and SILC to join forces and reduce duplication of effort. Although Title VII of the Rehab Act, as amended by WIOA, removed the requirement for the SRC representative from the SILC membership, under Title I, the SRC must include a SILC representative as a member so SILCs and SRCs still interface. At the end of the day, consumers benefit from these collaborations.

o Allows the SRCs to make more informed and better decisions.

o Provides the opportunity for collaboration and connection.

o Creates investment and buy-in.

o This is simply a good business practice.

Although this commitment and input will take more time in the beginning, this process will increase, with more accurate results. Collaboration and communication between all parties involved will help make this process flow more smoothly.

The needs assessment process includes several key steps ~

☐ Gathering input from the public and stakeholders;

☐ Holding public forums or focus groups;

☐ Conducting interviews, sending out surveys, etc.

Include basic questions about the value of current initiatives, whether the respondent would like different issues to be worked on, and which activities should be expanded. If conducting telephone interviews, these are typically more in-depth conversations and specific information is needed, but they are time-consuming. Interviews are helpful when important relationships are at stake and can provide answers to questions generated from the initial assessment.

This can be useful to find a way to reconnect with needs assessment participants. You may learn what is happening from the assessment, but still not know why. When you ask questions, develop a way to drill down deeper to obtain more specific information and answers. Group forums can generate synergy and influence. People may bounce ideas off one another in community groups.

Generating a good turnout at public forums is challenging. Having more than one partner involved with the forum may help to increase attendance. There is a myriad of ways to conduct consumer forums with both specific questions and open space where consumers get to pick topics and spend as much or as little time as they want talking about those topics, while having designated areas where pertinent information is given. Location of public forums is also a stumbling block especially in rural areas with no public transportation.

Social Media

The use of social media is an independent decision of each Council. Many Councils have elected to have an independent web page noting their Council's activities; while other Councils are part of their agency's web page. What you choose to include is once again a Council's decision.

Make sure when using social media to keep information current and interesting. Have contact information visible. The site should also be accessible.

Examples of websites for states and territories may be accessed on the NCSRC website under the "Members" heading at www.ncsrc.net. There is an increasing use of social media and this may be of benefit for your Council.

Appendix A: Example Conflict of Interest Policy/Statement and Code of Ethics

Conflict of Interest Policy

SRC members and employees are expected to support the work of the Council and to refrain from actions doing anything that would interfere with the success of the SRC. SRC members and employees have an obligation to conduct business within guidelines that prohibit actual or potential conflicts of interest. SRC members and employees should not provide any information to a competitor (an entity competing for the same grant, contract, etc.) that would adversely affect the SRC's success in its endeavors.

Likewise, SRC members and employees should not take advantage of opportunities for personal gain when dealing with grantees, suppliers, customers, etc. Any SRC member or employee that has a concern that a conflict of interest is present or may appear to be present, should inform the executive director or chairperson immediately.

An individual may not be hired for, or continue in, a position that is supervised by a member of that person's immediate family. Should a promotion or marriage occur that would result in this being the case, the two employees will be required to determine which will resign from employment with the SRC. If the employees are unable to make such determination within a reasonable amount of time, the employee with the shorter tenure will be terminated. Similarly, no SRC Council member or members of their families may be a paid employee of the SRC. This conflict of interest policy is designed to foster public confidence in the SRC and to protect the SRC's interest.

This policy establishes only the framework within which the SRC will operate. The purpose is to provide general direction and SRC members and employees are expected to seek further clarification from the Chairperson or Executive Director on issues related to the subject of acceptable standards of operation if any question arises.

SRC members and employees involved in the procurement/purchasing and/or decision-making processes are expected to disclose any potential conflict of interest and to remove themselves from the discussion and decision-making for any item of business in which they have a conflict of interest. No "presumption of guilt" is created by the mere existence of a relationship with an outside firm or individual. However, when an SRC member or employee has any influence on transactions involving purchases, contracts, or leases, it is imperative that disclosure of the existence of any actual or potential conflicts of interest be made to the Chairperson/full board or Executive Director as soon as possible so that safeguards can be implemented to protect all parties. Personal gain is prohibited.

Transactions are prohibited where the SRC member or employee, partner or relative has significant ownership in a firm with which the SRC does business. Any kickback, bribe, substantial gift, or special consideration to an individual or relative is prohibited as a result of any transaction or business dealings involving the SRC in which the individual has interest.

When a conflict of interest occurs, if a more advantageous option is not reasonably possible, the Council shall determine by a majority vote of members without a conflict of interest whether the option creating the conflict is in the SRC's best interest and whether it is fair and reasonable. Any SRC member or employee found guilty of an undisclosed conflict will be subject to
disciplinary action.

The SRC will document, in detailed minutes, any decisions related to a transaction involving an actual or potential conflict of interest. Actual or potential conflicts of interest involving federally funded activities must be reported to the federal awarding agency

Appendix B: Sample of Conflict of Interest Signature Form

This statement is to be completed annually by all SRC members and staff.

Name: _____ **Date:** _____

Position:

( ) Voting SRC member
( ) Ex-Officio, Non-Voting SRC member
( ) Officer: _____
( ) Staff member: _____
( ) Executive Director

I affirm that:

- I have received a copy of the SRC Conflict of Interest Policy. ___ **(initial)**
- I have read and understand the policy. ____ **(initial)**
- I agree to comply with the policy. ___ **(initial)**
- I understand that SRC is a charitable organization and in order to maintain the federal tax exempt status much engage in activities which accomplish one or more tax exempt purposes. ___ **(initial)**

Disclosures:

Please certify below any conflicts or potential conflicts or that you have nothing to report.

_____ I have the following current or potential conflicts in financial matters of the SRC (provide details).

_____ I have no current or potential conflicts to report at this time.

By my signature below I verify that the above information is true and correct to the best of my knowledge.

_____   _____
Signature   Date

Appendix C: Sample for Membership Handbook Sections

1   Mission, Vision, Purpose & History of the SRC

2   Membership Roster
        Membership Application

3   Council Committees & Responsibilities

4   Meeting Schedule

5   Bylaws
        Policies & Procedures

6   DRS State Plan

7   SRC Annual Reports
        SRC Consumer Satisfaction Survey & Letter

        Survey Report

8   Council Meeting Minutes

9   Executive Director Reports

10   Rehabilitation Act of 1973 Info

11   NCSRC

12   DRS Information

13   Travel Forms

14   Acronyms & Terminology

15   Miscellaneous

Appendix D: Sample of Draft of SRC Monthly Activity Schedule

JANUARY

- Executive Committee Conference Call
- Have Annual Report Printed
- Disseminate Annual Report
- Submit monthly grant billing to DRS

FEBRUARY

- Council Meeting - February
- Plan Council Legislative Visits
- Present State Plan Questions
- Begin Membership Campaign
- Review DRS Legislative Report
- Determine which members will attend Spring NCSRC/CSAVR events
- Submit monthly grant billing to DRS

MARCH

- Executive Committee Conference Call
- Discuss potential new Council members with VR Director
- Submit monthly grant billing to DRS

APRIL

- Council Meeting - April
- Recommend & Approve New Council Members
- Presentation from Consultant on Consumer Satisfaction Survey Report
- Submit monthly grant billing to DRS

MAY

- Executive Committee Conference Call
- Submit monthly grant billing to DRS

JUNE

- Council Meeting – June
- Discuss Planning Retreat
- Council Group Pic for Annual Report
- Bylaws Review
- Initiate Letter to DRS & Governor for New Member Approval
- Submit monthly grant billing to DRS

JULY

- Order & Organize New Member Manuals & Handbooks
- Executive Committee Conference Call
- Provide DRS Administration with List of New Members
- Submit monthly grant billing to DRS

AUGUST

- Council Meeting – August
- Determine Theme for Annual Report
- Gather quotes for Annual Report
- Begin Taking Necessary Pictures for Annual Report
- Election of Officers

- Pre-set Schedule for Meetings & Conference Calls for next FY
- New Officers Sign Signature Cards (Bank Accounts & Credit Card)
- Determine who will attend Fall NCSRC & CSAVR conference
- Update Website Information with agency staff
- Provide DRS Administration with List of New Members & Officers
- Submit monthly grant billing to DRS

SEPTEMBER

- Executive Committee Conference Call – To Be Announced
- Sign new grant agreement with agency
- Submit monthly grant billing to DRS

OCTOBER

- Council Meeting – October
- Sign-up for New Committees, chairpersons & dates of meetings
- Send Schedule of Meetings to all members & pertinent agency staff
- Schedule New Forums
- Continue Getting Any Pictures Needed for Annual Report
- Orientation of New Members
- New Members Complete Personal Information Data (for emergencies)
- Submit monthly grant billing to DRS

NOVEMBER

- Executive Committee Conference Call – To Be Announced
- Have audit or compilation report of finances
- Send schedule of the next year's meetings & conference room requests to necessary venues
- Draft annual report
- Get figures from agency needed for Annual Report\
- Submit monthly grant billing to DRS

DECEMBER

- Council Meeting – December
- Register with Secretary of State's Office Schedule of the next year's meetings
- Determine Legislative Priorities with DRS
- Annual Report Draft reviewed by Committee
- Annual Report sent to printer
- Performance Review of Executive Director
- Review Policy & Procedure Status
- Submit monthly grant billing to DRS
- Submit Annual Report to RSA by December 31st

Appendix E: Sample of Draft SRC Meeting Agenda

Conference Call-in Information
(555) 555-5555
Participant Number 555555#
Chair or SRC Director's cell   (555) 555-5555

Draft State Rehabilitation Council
Agenda
Meeting Date

Mission Statement

The State Rehabilitation Council is to review, analyze and advise the Division of Rehabilitation Services regarding its program eligibility, performance and effectiveness in empowering individuals with disabilities to achieve their employment goals.

9:00 a.m.	Welcome & Introductions Open Forum	Chairperson
9:15 a.m.	State of the Agency Fair Hearings Report	Agency VR Director
9:30 a.m.	Policies Update	Agency Person
9:45 a.m.	WIOA Performance Benchmarks Consumer Satisfaction	Agency Person
10:30 a.m.	Select Agency Program Presentation to Educate Council Members	Agency Person
Noon	Working Lunch	
1:00 a.m.	Secretary's Report Treasurer's Report Executive Director's Report	Council Secretary Council Treasurer SRC Staff Person
1:45 p.m.	NCSRC Conference Report	Member(s) who attended
2:15 p.m.	SILC Report	SILC Chairperson
2:00 p.m.	Old & New Business Upcoming NCSRC Conference Committee Reports as needed Announcements & Comments	Chairperson SRC Staff or Chairperson Committee Chairperson Chairperson
3:00 p.m.	Adjourn	

Appendix F: Sample of Draft List Preparing for Council Meetings

<u>TWO (2) OR THREE (3) WEEKS PRIOR TO MEETING</u>

- ✓ Work with Chairperson & agency staff to determine meeting agenda

- ✓ Send meeting notice to statewide media 3 weeks prior to meeting

- ✓ Notify Council members two (2) weeks prior to the scheduled meeting by e-mail, mail and/or telephone of the meeting date(s) requesting response form to be completed & returned

- ✓ E-mail, mail and/or record meeting materials (minutes, reports or other information) to members for their review two (2) weeks prior to the meeting – include agency director, pertinent agency staff & support staff, guest handouts as available in this

- ✓ Secure interpreters, as needed

- ✓ Confirm meeting room(s)

- ✓ Ask committee chairpersons for any written reports

<u>ONE WEEK PRIOR TO MEETING</u>

- ✓ Check with Council Chair & agency staff for verification of agenda

- ✓ Contact any out of town member to verify need for hotel reservations

- ✓ Make hotel reservations & send confirmation to hotel(s)

- ✓ Order break and lunch foods for working meeting

- ✓ Send financial reports to Chairperson & Treasurer for review prior to sending to members

- ✓ E-Mail Treasurer Transaction by Detail

- ✓ After approval of Chair & Treasurer e-mail financials to Executive Committee

- ✓ Distribute any agenda change info to Council members

✓ Make copies of travel & consultant forms for member to complete

✓ Confirm scheduled DRS or guest speakers for upcoming meeting

✓ Forward agenda to whomever is scheduled speaker

✓ Confirm interpreters if needed

Day Prior to Meeting Day

✓ Confirm food order & delivery time (if required)

✓ Gather supplies for meeting
  ➢ member name plates
  ➢ member travel forms
  ➢ tape recorder & blank tapes
  ➢ book containing meeting minutes
  ➢ copies of last month's minutes, current agenda, Executive Director report & financials statements
  ➢ blue ink pens
  ➢ any handouts
  ➢ flip chart & pens
  ➢ computer & power points
  ➢ camera
  ➢ eating utensils – napkins – drinks - supplies (if needed)

✓ Verify speaker times with speaker

Meeting Day

✓ Take all supplies to conference room

✓ Take blank check for miscellaneous

✓ Assure room set up

✓ Have conference call availability

✓ Make sure room has a flip chart available

✓ Have printed agendas for meeting

✓ Gather all folders from Council prior to the end of the meeting

✓ *Have interpreters complete their invoice and pay their expenses*

✓ *Clean up conference room*

Within Two Weeks Following the Meeting

✓ *Pay Council travel expenses*

✓ *Type minutes & forward to Council Secretary for additions or corrections*

✓ *Do any follow-ups with committees as directed from the meeting*

✓ *Verify hotel invoices received*

Appendix G: Sample of *Conference Calls*

Conference calls may occur due to inclement weather, committee meetings or when the Council must take action between regularly scheduled meetings.

- ✓ Councils should establish a toll-free conference call account that is available 24/7 with a minimum of 4 hours conferencing time per call.

- ✓ Once the time of the conference call has been determined, members and/or VR staff will be notified via email or text messaging.

- ✓ As much notice as possible of the scheduled call will be given at the request of the Council Chairperson, Executive Director or Agency management.

- ✓ An agenda & any written materials needed for the call will be e-mailed to participants prior to the conference call when time allows.

- ✓ The Council Secretary and/or Executive Director will record the call and disperse the minutes of the call to the participants.

- ✓ Council members unable to attend a Council meeting may call into regularly scheduled meetings.

- ✓ The call-in information should be clearly noted on the meeting agenda.

- ✓ Members should contact the Chairperson and/or SRC staff to designate they will be using the conferencing service prior to the start of the meeting.

Appendix H: Member Knowledge Checklist

What Every Member Should Know

A Self-Administered Test

The list below includes basic information that each member of a State Rehabilitation Council should know and understand to be an effective voting member of a statewide planning body.

If you are an SRC member and do not know about the issues listed below, you or your SRC may need training to learn and apply this knowledge in your role as a SRC member. Assess your knowledge of the following, writing "YES" or a "Y" for each statement you know and understand and a "NO" or an "N" for statements describing knowledge you do not yet have or fully understand. Be tough minded!

1. _____ The history of SRC related to and including the current Rehabilitation Act Amendments of 2014, particularly Section 105.

2. _____ The basic concepts, definitions, and protections of the Americans with Disabilities Act of 1990.

3. _____ The history of how the SRC developed in the United States.

4. _____ The SRC philosophy ~ its tenets, principles, values and how this is practiced.

5. _____ Conscious of the role of the SRC and the relationship with VR.

6. _____ Involved with the development, dissemination and responses of the Consumer Satisfaction Survey.

7. _____ The state agencies providing services to persons with disabilities, their missions, general information about what they provide, and their relationships to each other and within state government.

8. _____ Why partnering with other agencies who provide services for people disabilities is vital to what VR does and the connection with the SRC.

9. _____ The state's allocation for the SRC and how such funds are dispensed.

10. _____ Involved in the writing of observations and recommendations of the Unified or Combined State Plan, receives VR responses on the recommendations and any corrective action required from RSA.

11. _____ Understands the process used for gathering data for the WIOA Performance Benchmarks the Agency should achieve.

12. _____ Are the Council appointments compliant with the requirements in the law.

13. _____ Know the individual members of the SRC, who they represent on the SRC, their offices or responsibilities, if any, and how to reach any member of the SRC.

14. _____ The roles, responsibilities, and authority of each member of the SRC.

15. _____ Is given the opportunity during Council meetings for clarification, definition, assurances, and status of programs & services when asked of the Agency staff.

16. _____ Agency director provides in depth report at each Council meeting on the overall agency, including fiscal status, legislation, major issues and answers questions from members.

17. _____ The SRC is a federally mandated policy partner who works with the VR agency in developing policy and procedures.

18. _____ There is an effective and reliable communication system established for your SRC.

19. _____ The articles of incorporation (if appropriate), bylaws, or other tools of governance or policy guidance used by the SRC are given to each member.

20. _____ The committee structure of the Council is active and productive.

21. _____ Meetings are interactive and items on the agenda are discussed with a sense of accomplishment.

22. _____ Know the budget guiding SRC expenditures, the source(s) of SRC funding, and how such fiscal matters are managed.

23. _____ The staff of the SRC is accessible, staff relates to the individual members of the SRC & has a good working relationship with VR management & staff.

24. _____ How staff of the SRC are trained, supervised and evaluated.

25. _____ Kept abreast of SRC involvement with National Coalition of State Rehabilitation Councils (NCSRC) and Council of State Administrators of Vocational Rehabilitation (CSAVR).

www.ingramcontent.com/pod-product-compliance
Lightning Source LLC
Chambersburg PA
CBHW081750220526
45468CB00008B/2319